Bunbhó, a chuar,

LÁ BREITHE SHONA DUIT SWEETHEART

Samhain 2007

- 21 -

Níos fhaidhúine fásh anois thú & súil agam go mbíonn
breithlá & téisív dean scoth agat & go dtuitníonn do lluránteen
leat. Bhí mé ag smaoineamh ar chonas iontpáraid's spreagach
oilhreachb a fhsbhairt duit leallee. Guo wife os do choirdeast
fach mó thar na bliunta. Gro ollwhar's scanai

xoxoxoxoxoxoxox

Cool Hotels
Ecological

teNeues

Editor: Patricia Massó
Editorial coordination: Hanna Martin
Editorial assistance: Hanna Engelmeier, Katharina Feuer, Christiane Niemann
Introduction: Bärbel Holzberg
Translations: Star Deutschland GmbH, Böblingen
Layout & Pre-press: Jasmina Bremer
Imaging: Jan Hausberg

Produced by fusion publishing GmbH, Stuttgart . Los Angeles   www.fusion-publishing.com

Special Thanks to Anke Schaffelhuber and Wilderness Safaris for their expert advise and to
Bea Wolfe, Christine McCann, Tania Lee, Simone Rathle, Alex Withers, Nicole Merse, Lincoln
Hoffman, Bob Gevinski, Michael Franco, Karolin Troubetzkoy, Daniel Mellado, Emma Sartie,
Neil Rogers, Maria J. Barquero, Gustavo Castaing, Simon Heyes, Claire André de Cerff,
Isabell Schreml, Valeria Peroni, Holly Elizabeth Worton, Abdullah Inal, Johannes Auer, Paolo
Kastelec, Barbara Aster, Britta Ploenzke, Alicia Fernandez, Mike McHugo, Marit Meineke,
Kirsten Beck, Valeri Senekal, Helen Schröger, Ingo Jacob, Juliet Agg-Manning, Stephan R.
Brueckner, Benjamin Parker, Grant Cumings, Vanessa Hauser, Deborah Ewing, Bettina Faust,
Barbara Lueers, Anjali Nihalchand, Scott Crouch, Damien Hanger, Alana Saphin, Katherine
Paterson

Published by teNeues Publishing Group

teNeues Verlag GmbH+Co.KG
International Sales Division
Speditionstraße 17
40221 Düsseldorf, Germany
Tel.: 0049-(0)211-994597-0
Fax: 0049-(0)211-994597-40
E-mail: books@teneues.de

teNeues Publishing Company
16 West 22nd Street
New York, NY 10010, USA
Tel.: 001-212-627-9090
Fax: 001-212-627-9511

teNeues Publishing UK Ltd.
P.O. Box 402
West Byfleet
KT14 7ZF, Great Britain
Tel.: 0044-1932-403509
Fax: 0044-1932-403514

teNeues France S.A.R.L.
4, rue de Valence
75005 Paris, France
Tel.: 0033-1-55766205
Fax: 0033-1-55766419

teNeues Ibérica S.L.
c/Velázquez, 57 6.° izda.
28001 Madrid, Spain
Tel.: 0034-657-132133

teNeues
Representative Office Italy
Via San Vittore 36/1
20123 Milano, Italy
Tel.: 0039-(0)347-7640551

Press department: arehn@teneues.de
Phone: 0049-2152-916-202

www.teneues.com

ISBN-10: 3-8327-9135-3
ISBN-13: 978-3-8327-9135-3

Bibliographic information published by Die Deutsche Bibliothek.
Die Deutsche Bibliothek lists this publication in the Deutsche Nationalbibliografie;
detailed bibliographic data is available in the Internet at http://dnb.ddb.de

Content

Europe

Africa & Middle East

Asia & Pacific

Introduction

It was not long ago that the terms "ecologically-sound" and "design" seemed to be mutually exclusive. Anything labeled "eco-friendly" was usually handmade, plant-dyed, and inelegant, or at least somewhat insipid, and therefore the complete opposite of "cool". Hardcore ecologists rejected aesthetics, clarity, and the vibrant relationship between form and function—in short, all the qualities we associate with sophisticated contemporary design. Now all that has changed. Our planet is under threat and ecological awareness and eco-friendly living have become hot topics all over the world. Lifestyle-oriented urban dwellers have discovered themes such as sustainability and environmental soundness. This is a trend that carries over to vacation choices. Travelers are selecting eco-hotels that feature contemporary design.

The hotels presented in this book were not selected based on a checklist that may result in an ecological seal of approval based on points awarded. The hotels are special because they are designed to blend into the natural landscape and conserve natural resources. This starts with the building materials selected. Stone or renewable materials such as wood are often used. These are materials that would normally be used locally for building. Many hotels forego energy-guzzling air conditioning. In southern countries, buildings are carefully positioned to create as much shade as possible. Windows are installed in positions that allow continuous air circulation. Wherever possible, these eco-

hotels use renewable energy sources such as solar and wind power and minimize the amount of garbage they produce. This is an important issue particularly in regions such as the Maldives, where garbage disposal poses an enormous challenge.

Nature is always at the center of the hotels presented in this book. The transitions from indoors to outdoors are fluid, providing guests with a true experience of nature while preserving its appeal for generations to come.

Bärbel Holzberg

Einleitung

Es ist noch nicht lange her, da schienen sich die beiden Begriffe Öko und Design auszuschließen. Alles was unter dem Label Öko firmierte, kam handgemacht, pflanzengefärbt und unförmig, zumindest aber immer etwas freudlos, kurz, durch und durch uncool daher. Ästhetik, Klarheit, eine spannungsvolle Beziehung von Form und Funktion – eben was wir mit anspruchsvollem zeitgemäßem Design verbinden, wurde von überzeugten Ökofans abgelehnt. Das hat sich grundlegend geändert. Angesichts der Bedrohung unseres Planeten sind ökologisches Bewusstsein und Handeln zu globalisierten Massenthemen geworden. Nun sind es lifestyleorientierte Großstädter, die Begriffe wie Nachhaltigkeit und Umweltverträglichkeit für sich entdeckt haben. Ein Trend, der auch in den Ferien gelebt werden will, und in Öko-Hotels, die zeitgemäß gestaltet sind, seine Entsprechung findet.

Die Hotels in dem Buch wurden nicht mittels einer Checkliste ausgewählt, auf der nach Punktevergabe quasi ein Ökosiegel vergeben wird. Sie zeichnen sich durch das Konzept aus, sich organisch in die Landschaft einzufügen und die natürlichen Ressourcen zu schonen. Das beginnt schon mit den Baumaterialien. Als solche dienen oft Stein oder nachwachsende Stoffe wie Holz. Alles Materialien, mit denen auch sonst in der Region gebaut wird. Vielfach wird auf energiefressende Klimaanlagen verzichtet. Das funktioniert auch in südlichen Ländern durch die sinnvolle Positionierung der Gebäude zur Schaffung von Schattenquellen oder durch die geschickte Anlage von Fenstern, die

ständige Luftzirkulation bewirken. Die ökologischen Hotels nutzen, wenn möglich, erneuerbare Energiequellen wie Sonnen- und Windkraft und versuchen Abfall zu vermeiden. Ein wichtiges Thema, besonders in Regionen wie den Malediven, wo die Müllbeseitigung eine riesige Herausforderung darstellt.

Bei den vorgestellten Hotels darf immer die Natur die Hauptrolle spielen. Die Übergänge von innen und außen sind fließend. Dies ermöglicht den Gästen ein unverfälschtes Naturerlebnis, ohne damit die Reize der Natur für künftige Generationen zu zerstören.

Bärbel Holzberg

Introduction

Il n'y a pas si longtemps encore, les concepts d'écologie et de design semblaient ne pas pouvoir aller de pair. Tous les produits parés du label écologique étaient faits main, à base de colorants végétaux, ternes et de forme peu esthétique : ils étaient loin, par conséquent, de susciter l'enthousiasme auprès des adeptes du design. Le côté esthétique, épuré, l'intensité du lien entre la forme et la fonction de l'objet – tout ce qui justement caractérise le design moderne et raffiné – étaient vivement rejetés par les écologistes convaincus. Aujourd'hui, cette tendance s'est totalement inversée. Face à la menace qui plane sur notre bonne vieille planète, la prise de conscience écologique et les actions à mener dans ce domaine ont acquis une dimension mondiale. Désormais, les grandes métropoles adeptes du « Lifestyle » redécouvrent et s'approprient les concepts de développement durable et de respect de l'environnement. Une tendance également revendiquée et recherchée par de nombreux vacanciers qui trouvent leur bonheur dans les hôtels écologiques au design tout à fait moderne.

Les hôtels présentés dans cet ouvrage n'ont pas été sélectionnés à partir d'une liste de critères attribuant le label « écologique » en fonction du nombre de points obtenus. Non, ces hôtels se distinguent par un concept : se fondre dans le paysage tout en ménageant les ressources naturelles. À commencer par les matériaux utilisés pour leur construction : la pierre bien souvent, ou des matières premières renouvelables, comme le bois. Les mêmes matériaux que ceux

généralement utilisés dans la région. Les climatiseurs, très gourmands
en énergie, sont souvent absents de ces hôtels. On parvient en effet
à se passer de climatisation, même dans les pays méridionaux, grâce
au positionnement étudié des bâtiments qui privilégie les espaces
ombragés et aux fenêtres équipées pour laisser l'air circuler librement
en permanence. Lorsque les conditions le permettent, les hôtels
écologiques utilisent des sources d'énergie renouvelables (énergies
solaire et éolienne) et tentent de limiter la production de déchets.
Un objectif important, notamment dans des régions comme les îles
Maldives où l'élimination des déchets relève d'un véritable défi.
Les hôtels présentés dans cet ouvrage redonnent une place essentielle
à la nature. On passe très facilement de l'intérieur à l'extérieur. Ainsi,
les hôtes bénéficient d'une relation authentique avec la nature et tout le
charme de celle-ci est préservé pour les générations à venir.

Bärbel Holzberg

Introducción

Hasta hace poco, los conceptos "ecología" y "diseño" parecían ser incompatibles. Todo lo que se incluía bajo la etiqueta "ecológico" estaba hecho a mano, teñido con pigmentos naturales, tenía formas poco armoniosas y casi siempre resultaba triste y aburrido. En resumen: tenía todos los puntos para resultar muy poco atractivo. Los más fieles seguidores de la ecología rechazaban el sentido estético, la claridad, la siempre excitante relación entre forma y función y, en definitiva, todo lo relacionado con el diseño más actual y exigente. Sin embargo, esto ha cambiado por completo. En vista de las numerosas amenazas que sufre nuestro planeta, la conciencia ecológica y las conductas respetuosas con el medio ambiente se han convertido en cuestiones de trascendencia internacional. En la actualidad, hay grandes ciudades que han incorporado a su estilo de vida conceptos como la sostenibilidad o el impacto ambiental. Se trata de una tendencia a la que algunas personas desean dar continuidad también durante sus vacaciones y que encuentra la respuesta idónea en hoteles ecológicos que, además, cuentan con el diseño más actual.

Los hoteles de este libro no se han seleccionado mediante la asignación de puntos para obtener un "certificado ecológico". Se trata de hoteles que se distinguen por la capacidad de integrarse de forma orgánica en el paisaje y de preservar los recursos naturales. Esto se aprecia incluso en los materiales con los que están construidos, que suelen ser la piedra o materias primas renovables como la madera. En definitiva,

los materiales con los que se construye en las regiones en las que están ubicados. Estos hoteles renuncian a las instalaciones de aire acondicionado, muy costosas en términos energéticos, y las suplen con ingeniosos sistemas que funcionan incluso en los países meridionales, en los que se estudia la adecuada orientación de los edificios para conseguir más zonas con sombra o la ubicación más acertada de las ventanas para generar corrientes de aire continuas. Siempre que sea posible, los hoteles ecológicos utilizan fuentes de energía renovables como el sol o la energía eólica y procuran minimizar la generación de residuos. Este último aspecto es clave sobre todo en regiones como por ejemplo las Maldivas, en las que la eliminación de residuos requiere un inmenso esfuerzo.

La naturaleza es la protagonista en todos los hoteles que presentamos. El intercambio entre el interior y el exterior se realiza con fluidez. De este modo, los huéspedes pueden disfrutar al máximo de la naturaleza sin destruir los tesoros que ésta depara a las generaciones futuras.

Bärbel Holzberg

Introduzione

Fino a non molto tempo fa, ecologia e design erano concetti che
si escludevano a vicenda; l'etichetta "ecologico", infatti, evocava
necessariamente l'idea di un prodotto fatto a mano, tinto con colori
naturali e senza una forma definita, richiamando quindi una sorta di
grigiore e monotonia intrinseci, qualcosa privo di fascino, insomma,
Dall'altra parte, estetica, linearità e antitesi tra forma e funzionalità,
da sempre, sono stati associati al design moderno dal carattere
pretenzioso, costantemente rifiutato dagli ecologisti più convinti.
Abbiamo tuttavia assistito ad una grande trasformazione: le minacce
che gravano sul nostro pianeta hanno plasmato le coscienze ed i
comportamenti comuni globalizzando i concetti relativi all'ambiente.
Persino gli abitanti delle grandi metropoli regine del lifestyle hanno
oggi riscoperto concetti importanti quali la conservazione delle risorse
e la sostenibilità. Una nuova tendenza che si vuole vivere anche in
vacanza e che trova la sua realizzazione negli ecohotel, costruiti con-
iugando design moderno ed ecologia.
Tutti gli hotel presentati in questo volume non sono stati recensiti in
base ad una graduatoria per l'assegnazione di eventuali riconoscimenti
ecologici, bensì si contraddistinguono per un nuovo concetto: l'inse-
rimento sapiente ed armonioso nel paesaggio circostante e la salva-
guardia delle risorse naturali. Questo inizia già dalla scelta dei materiali
da costruzione: spesso la pietra o materie rinnovabili come il legno, tutti
materiali caratteristici dell'architettura locale. Non è insolito, inoltre,

rinunciare alle fonti divoratrici di energia, quali gli impianti di condizionamento, a favore di soluzioni alternative, persino nelle aree più calde del sud. In queste zone, infatti, gli edifici vengono dislocati in posizioni strategiche tali da creare ombra e ripari oppure si ricorre ad ingegnosi sistemi di disposizione delle finestre per garantire così una circolazione continua dell'aria. Gli ecohotel sfruttano, ove possibile, le fonti di energia rinnovabili, quali l'energia solare ed eolica, e cercano di evitare la produzione di rifiuti. Aspetto, quest'ultimo, fondamentale soprattutto in quelle regioni, come le Maldive, dove lo smaltimento dei rifiuti rappresenta una sfida enorme.

In tutti questi hotel la natura è sempre posta in primo piano. Interni ed esterni si fondono in un tutt'uno per permettere agli ospiti di vivere un'esperienza di autentica immersione nella natura, pur preservandone il fascino straordinario anche per le generazioni future.

Bärbel Holzberg

Americas

California
Post Ranch Inn
El Capitan Canyon

New York
Lake Placid Lodge
The Point

Caribbean
Lone Star
Necker Island
Jake's
Goldeneye
The Caves
Montpelier Plantation Inn
Hix Island House, A Vieques Hotel
Anse Chastanet

Mexico
Hacienda San José
Hacienda Uayamón
Hotelito Desconocido

Belize
Turtle Inn

Guatemala
La Lancha

Costa Rica
Hotel Punta Islita

Peru
Machu Picchu Pueblo Hotel

Brazil
Pousada Picinguaba

Argentina
Don Enrique Lodge

Chile
Explora en Atacama

Post Ranch Inn

Address: Highway 1, P.O. Box 219, Big Sur, CA 93920, USA
Phone: +1 831 667 2200
Fax: +1 831 667 2824

Website: www.postranchinn.com
e-mail: reservations@postranchinn.com

Located: 30 minutes from Carmel and 45 minutes from Monterey
Style: natural minimalistic, eco style architecture
Special features: restaurant, swimming pool, spa, Shaman sessions, workout room, library
Rooms: 30 rooms, 2 houses

Opening date: 1992

Architecture / Design: Mickey Meunnig
Janet Gay-Freed

El Capitan Canyon

Address: 11560 Calle Real, Santa Barbara, CA 93117, USA
Phone: +1 866 352 2729
Fax: +1 805 968 6772

Website: www.elcapitancanyon.com
e-mail: info@elcapitancanyon.com

Located: 15 minutes north of Santa Barbara
Style: countrystyle with references to the history of the Canyon
Special features: swimming pool, yoga, water sports, horseback riding, hiking, biking, stargazing
Rooms: 100 cedar cabins, 26 classic safari tents

Opening date: 2001

Architecture / Design: Blackbird Architects Inc.

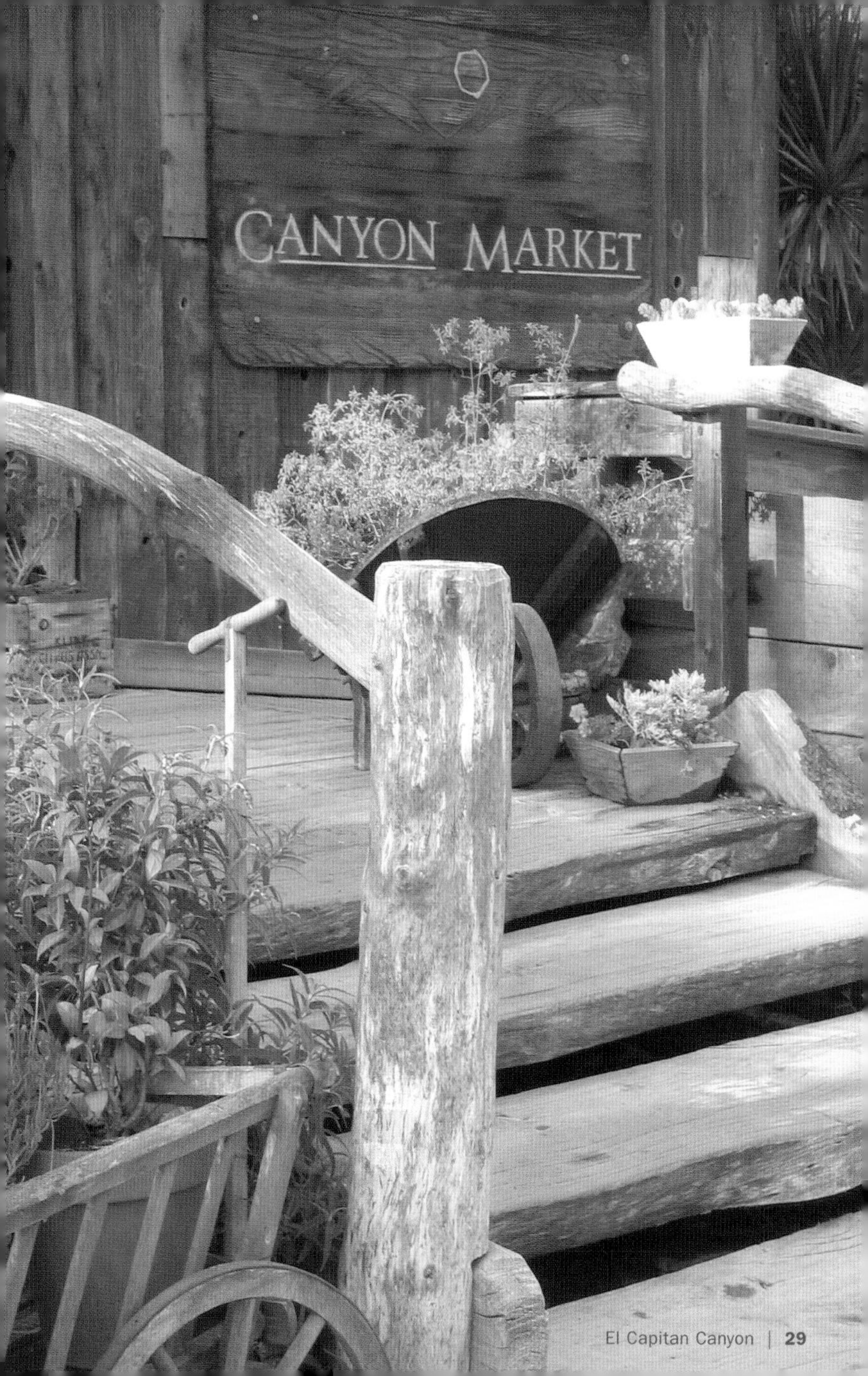
CANYON MARKET

Lake Placid Lodge

Address:	Whiteface Inn Road, P.O. Box 550, Lake Placid, NY 12946, USA
Phone:	+1 518 523 2700
Fax:	+1 518 523 1124
Website:	www.lakeplacidlodge.com
e-mail:	info@lakeplacidlodge.com
Located:	in the heart of the Adirondacks, 2 hours to Montreal, 5 hours to New York
Style:	rustic elegance in Adirondack style, originally built in 1882
Special features:	restaurant, spa, winter sports, golf, horseback riding, fishing
Rooms:	34 accommodations
Opening date:	1995
Architecture / Design:	Truex Cullins & Partners Architects

The Point

Address: P.O. Box 1327, Saranac Lake, NY 12983, USA
Phone: +1 518 891 5674
Fax: +1 518 891 1152

Website: www.thepointresort.com
e-mail: point@relaischateaux.com

Located: 6-hour drive to Manhattan, 3-hour drive to Montreal and 2.5-hour drive to Burlington
Style: Adirondack Great Camp architecture with an atmosphere of traditional country house party hospitality
Special features: boating, hiking, biking, horseback riding, fishing, winter sports, golf, hunting
Rooms: 11 rooms in 4 buildings

Opening date: 1986

Architecture / Design: William Distin, 1933
Christie Garrett and Joszi Meskan Associates

Lone Star

Address: St. James, Barbados
Phone: +1 246 419 0599
Fax: +1 246 419 0597

Website: www.thelonestar.com
e-mail: wowgroupltd@sunbeach.net

Located: at the west coast of Barbados with an ocean-front setting
Style: Caribbean style suites, natural minimalistic
Special features: paintings and antiques
Rooms: 4 suites

Opening date: 1997, originally constructed in the 1940's

Architecture / Design: Michael Pemberton

Necker Island

Address:	Necker Island, P.O. Box 1091, The Valley, Virgin Gorda, British Virgin Islands
Phone:	+1 284 494 2757
Fax:	+1 284 494 4396
Website:	www.virgin.com/subsites/necker
e-mail:	enquiries@limitededition.virgin.co.uk
Located:	15 minutes by boat to Virgin Gorda, 30 minutes from Beef Island/Tortola
Style:	Balinese style
Special features:	privat island with up to 26 guests, water sports, tennis, gym
Rooms:	10 rooms, 1 suite
Opening date:	1984
Architecture / Design:	Jon Osmon Linda Garland

Jake's

Address:	Calabash Bay, Treasure Beach, St. Elizabeth, Jamaica
Phone:	+1 876 965 3000
Fax:	+1 876 965 0552
Website:	www.islandoutpost.com
e-mail:	jakes@cwjamaica.com
Located:	on the south coast in Treasure Beach, 2 hours from Montego Bay Airport
Style:	Moroccan Casbah-style with contemporary design
Special features:	2 restaurants, biking, snorkeling, kayaking and deep-sea fishing, cookery courses
Rooms:	29 rooms in 15 cottages
Opening date:	1998
Architecture / Design:	Sally Henzell

Goldeneye

Address: Oracabessa, St. Mary, Jamaica
Phone: +1 876 975 3354
Fax: +1 876 975 3620

Website: www.islandoutpost.com
e-mail: goldeneye@cwjamaica.com

Located: 20 minutes from Ocho Rios, 2 hours from Montego Bay Airport
Style: natural flair with handcraft furniture
Special features: Ian Fleming wrote 17 of his James Bond books here. Spa, yoga, massages, tennis, water sports, art and craft classes, privat courtyards
Rooms: 120 cottages, suiten and villas

Opening date: re-opening December 2007

Architecture / Design: Anne Hodges
Barbara Hulanicki

The Caves

Address: P.O. Box 3113, Light House Road, Negril, Jamaica
Phone: +1 876 957 0270
Fax: +1 876 957 4930

Website: www.islandoutpost.com
e-mail: thecaves@cwjamaica.com

Located: Western Jamaica, 1.5 hour from the Montego Bay Airport
Style: handcrafted cottages made of wood and stone, roofed in thatch
Special features: a grotto designed for dining, spa
Rooms: 10 cottages

Opening date: 1997

Architecture / Design: Bertram Saulter
Greer-Ann Saulter

Montpellier Plantation Inn

Address:	P.O. Box 474 Nevis, West Indies
Phone:	+1 869 469 3462
Fax:	+1 869 469 2932
Website:	www.montpeliernevis.com
e-mail:	info@montpeliernevis.com
Located:	230 m above the Caribbean Sea on the island of Nevis
Style:	elegant Caribbean style, a former plantation from the 18th century
Special features:	2 restaurants, private beach, 20 meter pool. Arrangements off property: golf, spa treatments, water sports, hiking, horseback riding
Rooms:	15 rooms and 1 suite
Opening date:	2002
Architecture / Design:	Tonya & Muffin Hoffman and Martynne Kupciunas of Fine Line Interiors

Hix Island House, A Vieques Hotel

Address: HC-02 Box 14902, Vieques, Puerto Rico 00765
Phone: +1 787 741 2302
Fax: +1 787 741 2797

Website: www.hixislandhouse.com
e-mail: info@hixislandhouse.com

Located: five minutes from the Vieques Airport in Pilon
Style: Zen-inspired design with reference to the Japanese Wabi-Sabi concept
Special features: yoga, massage, fishing, sailing, kayaking, hiking, biking, horseback riding
Rooms: 13 suites in 4 buildings

Opening date: 1986

Architecture / Design: John Hix Architect

Hix Island House, A Vieques Hotel | **83**

Anse Chastanet

Address: P.O. Box 7000, Soufriere, St. Lucia
Phone: 758 459 7000
Fax: 758 459 7700

Website: www.ansechastanet.com
e-mail: ansechastanet@candw.lc

Located: 2.5 km to town, on a hillside overlooking Piton Mountains and the ocean
Style: handmade furnishings of regional woods
Special features: 100 stairs to the beach level, 2 restaurants and bars, 2 boutiques, spa, watersports center, art gallery, library
Rooms: 40 rooms on hillside and within tropical garden

Opening date: 1974, renovated in 2000

Architecture / Design: Nick Troubetzkoy

Hacienda San José

Address: KM 30 Carretera, Tixkokob-Tekanto, Tixkokob,
97470 Mexico
Phone: +52 999 910 4617
Fax: +52 999 923 7963

Website: www.haciendasmexico.com
e-mail: reservations1@thehaciendas.com

Located: Northern Yucatán peninsula, close to Chichén
Itzá, 38 km from Merida International Airport
Style: former plantation house in Colonial style
combined with Mayan and contemporary design
Special features: horseback riding, mountain biking, swimming
pool, library, archeological tours, spa treatments
and massages
Rooms: 15 rooms and suites

Opening date: re-done 1998

Architecture / Design: Plan arquitectos, Luis Bossoms

Hacienda Uayamón

Address: KM 20 Carretera, Uayamon-China-Edzna
Uayamon, Campeche, Mexico
Phone: +52 981 829 7527
Fax: +52 999 923 7963

Website: www.haciendasmexico.com
e-mail: reservations1@thehaciendas.com

Located: in the Yucatán peninsula, 26 km to Campeche,
2-hour drive to Merida International Airport
Style: Colonial style combined with contemporary
design
Special features: swimming pool, library, spa treatments
and massages, horseback riding, biking,
archeological tours
Rooms: 12 rooms and suites

Opening date: 2000

Architecture / Design: Plan arquitectos, Luis Bossoms

Hotelito Desconocido

Address: Playon de Mismaloya SN, La Cruz de Loreto-Tomatlán, Jalisco, Mexico
Phone: +52 322 281 4010
Fax: +52 322 281 4130

Website: www.hotelito.com
e-mail: hotelito@hotelito.com

Located: in a natural reserve located 90 km south of Puerto Vallarta
Style: romantic rustic eco style
Special features: 2 restaurants, bar, spa treatments and massages, jacuzzi, steam bath, yoga, beach, horseback riding, sea turtles release, bird-watching tours. No electricity and no phone
Rooms: 12 buildings on stilts and 12 beach bungalows

Opening date: 1996

Architecture / Design: Marcello Murzilli

Turtle Inn

Address: Placencia Village, Stann Creek District, Belize
Phone: +501 824 4912
Fax: +501 824 4913

Website: www.blancaneaux.com
e-mail: info@blancaneaux.com

Located: north of Placencia Village at the southern tip of the Placencia Peninsula on Belize's southern Caribbean coast
Style: Balinese inspired cottages and villas
Special features: 2 swimming pools, 3 restaurants, 2 bars, dive shop, Sunset Spa and Thai Massage Pavilion
Rooms: 25 rooms

Opening date: 2003

Architecture / Design: Francis Ford Coppola

La Lancha

Address: Lake Petén Itzá, Tikal, Guatemala
Phone: +501 824 4912
Fax: +501 824 4912

Website: www.lalancha.com
e-mail: info@blancaneaux.com

Located: 30-minute drive to the Mayan site of Tikal, in north-eastern Guatemala
Style: design influenced by Balinese and Guatemalan styles
Special features: restaurant, bar, swimming pool
Rooms: 10 casitas

Opening date: 2005

Architecture / Design: interior design by Eleanor Coppola and Francis Ford Coppola

Hotel Punta Islita

Address:	Hotel Punta Islita, Guanacaste, Costa Rica
Phone:	+506 231 6122
Fax:	+506 231 0715
Website:	www.hotelpuntaislita.com
e-mail:	info@hotelpuntaislita.com
Located:	on the north-west coast of Guanacaste on the peninsula of Nicoya, 30-minute flight or 4.5-hour drive to San Jose
Style:	rustic-colonial architecture
Special features:	fitness center, gym, jacuzzi, sauna, hiking, kayaking, fishing, mountain biking, horseback riding
Rooms:	33 rooms
Opening date:	1994
Architecture / Design:	Ronald Zürcher, ZÜRCHER ARQUITECTOS

Don Enrique Lodge

Address: From Buenos Aires, M. Santana 261 (1642)
San Isidro Buenos Aires, Argentina
Phone: +54 114 723 7020

Website: www.donenriquelodge.com.ar
e-mail: info@donenriquelodge.com.ar

Located: in the center-east of Misiones Province located
280 km to Posadas and 290 km to the Iguazu
Falls
Style: simple rustic decoration built with wood from the
area
Special features: restaurant, guided hikes in the woods, swimming
in the Paraíso river, fishing
Rooms: 3 cabins, one suite room

Opening date: 2005

Architecture / Design: Guillermo Di Renzo (architecture)
Gustavo y Malena Castaing (interior)

Pousada Picinguaba

Address:	Rua G, 130, Vila Picinguaba, 11680-000 Ubatuba-Sp, Brazil
Phone:	+55 123 836 9105
Fax:	+55 123 836 9103
Website:	www.picinguaba.com
e-mail:	info@picinguaba.com
Located:	overlooking a bay in protected Mata Atlantica rainforest, a 30-minute drive from colonial town of Parati
Style:	contemporary tropical style
Special features:	swimming pool, library, piano
Rooms:	10 rooms including 1 suite
Opening date:	2002
Architecture / Design:	Emmanuel Rengade Cristina Andrade Furtado (landscape design)

Machu Picchu Pueblo Hotel

Address:	Machu Picchu Km 110, Machu Picchu, 999 Peru
Phone:	+51 8421 1039
Fax:	+51 8421 1124
Website:	www.inkaterra.com
e-mail:	central@inkaterra.com
Located:	in the heart of Machu Picchu Historical Sanctuary
Style:	handcrafted architecture in Andean style
Special features:	restaurants, boutique, bar, chapel, spring water bathing pool, orchid garden
Rooms:	85 rooms and suites
Opening date:	1991
Architecture / Design:	Denise Koechlin

Explora en Atacama

Address: Ayllu de Larache, Casilla 8, San Pedro de Atacama, Chile
Phone: +56 2206 6060
Fax: +56 2228 4655

Website: www.explora.com
e-mail: reservexplora@explora.com

Located: in 2,500 m high in the Atacama desert, 1-hour drive to Calama, 2.5-hour flight from Santiago
Style: Atacama Indian style, puristic, light-flooded
Special features: restaurant, lobby, swimming pool, guided excursions, gallery
Rooms: 50 rooms and suites

Opening date: 1998

Architecture / Design: Germán del Sol

Europe

Turkey
Austria
Italy
Spain

Austria
Naturhotel Waldklause

Italy
Villa Fontelunga
Vigilius Mountain Resort

Spain (Majorca)
Ca'n Verdera
Ca's Xorc
Son Bernadinet
Son Gener

Turkey
Yunak Evleri

Yunak Evleri

Address:	Yunak Mahallesi 50400, Urgup, Cappadocia, Turkey
Phone:	+ 90 384 341 6920
Fax:	+ 90 384 341 6924
Website:	www.yunak.com
e-mail:	yunak@yunak.com
Located:	in the center of Urgup, in the area of Cappadoci
Style:	carved into a mountain cliff, Mediterranean style
Special features:	restaurant, hot air ballooning, trekking, biking, horseback riding, library, music room, conferenc facilities up to 60 people
Rooms:	17 rooms in 6 houses
Opening date:	1999
Architecture / Design:	Cavit Kartal

Naturhotel Waldklause

Address: Unterlängenfeld 190, 6444 Längenfeld, Austria
Phone: +43 5253 5455
Fax: +43 5253 54554

Website: www.waldklause.at
e-mail: office@waldklause.at

Located: in Oetz Valley in Längenfeld, a popular ski resor
in Tyrol, next to thermal springs
Style: contemporary ecological style in wood, glass an
stone
Special features: winter and summer sports, steam bath, sauna,
herbal sauna
Rooms: 46 rooms

Opening date: 2004

Architecture / Design: Markus Kastl

Villa Fontelunga

Address: Via Cunicchio No. 5, Loc. Pozzo, Foiano della
Chiana, 52045 Arezzo, Tuscany, Italy
Phone: +39 057 566 0410
Fax: +39 057 566 1963

Website: www.fontelunga.com
e-mail: info@fontelunga.com

Located: 1 hour from Firenze, 2 hours from Rome
Style: traditional Tuscan style and contemporary design
Special features: swimming pool, tennis court on site,
facilities for weddings
Rooms: 9 rooms

Opening date: 2000

Architecture / Design: Philip Robinson

Vigilius Mountain Resort

Address: Vigiljoch Mountain, 39011 Lana, Italy
Phone: +39 047 355 6600
Fax: +39 047 355 6699

Website: www.vigilius.it
e-mail: info@vigilius.it

Located: 1,500 m above sea level, 7 km from Merano
Style: ecological and organic style with wood and glass
Special features: restaurant, "Stube", wine cellar, spa, indoor pool, whirlpool, sauna, steam bath, flexible meeting room for up to 40 people
Rooms: 35 rooms, 6 suites

Opening date: 2003

Architecture / Design: Matteo Thun

vigilius

Ca'n Verdera

Address: Carrer des Toros, 1, 07109 Fornalutx, Spain
Phone: +34 971 638 203
Fax: +34 971 638 109

Website: www.canverdera.com
e-mail: info@canverdera.com

Located: at the west coast of Majorca, 50 km from Palma
Style: 150-year-old building of stone, Majorcan-Mediterranean style
Special features: restaurant, bar, swimming pool, conference room for up to 24 people
Rooms: 4 rooms, 2 suites

Opening date: 1998

Architecture / Design: Pepe Frontera

Ca's Xorc

Address: Carreta de Deia, km 56.1, 07100 Sóller, Spain
Phone: +34 971 638 280
Fax: +34 971 632 949

Website: www.casxorc.com
e-mail: stay@casxorc.com

Located: in the north west of Majorca
Style: traditional finca, a former oil press, in Majorcan Mediterranean style
Special features: restaurant, swimming pool, jacuzzi
Rooms: 12 rooms

Opening date: 2000

Architecture / Design: Wolfgang Nikolaus Schmidt
Mariano Barcelo
Juan & Gregory Puigserver

Son Bernadinet

Address:	Carretera Campos-Porreras, km 5.9, 07630 Campos, Spain
Phone:	+34 971 650 694
Fax:	+34 971 651 340
Website:	www.son-bernadinet.com
e-mail:	info@son-bernadinet.com
Located:	in the south of Majorca, 40 km from Palma
Style:	Majorcan-Mediterranean style
Special features:	swimming pool, musician room, flower and vegetable gardens
Rooms:	11 rooms
Opening date:	1998
Architecture / Design:	Antonio Esteva

Son Bernadinet | **213**

Son Gener

Address:	Caretera Vieja Son Servera – Artà, km 3, 07550 Son Servera, Spain
Phone:	+34 971 183 612
Fax:	+34 971 183 591
Website:	www.songener.com
e-mail:	hotel@songener.com
Located:	on a hill in the east of Majorca, 70 km from Palma
Style:	Majorcan-Mediterranean style, a former 18th-century farmhouse
Special features:	restaurant, wine cellar, swimming pool, spa, hammam, jacuzzi, yoga, gym, terrace
Rooms:	10 suites
Opening date:	1998
Architecture / Design:	Antonio Esteva

Africa & Middle East

Morocco
UAE
Seychelles
Kenya
Tanzania
Botswana
Malawi
Mozambique
Namibia
Zambia
Zimbabwe
South Africa

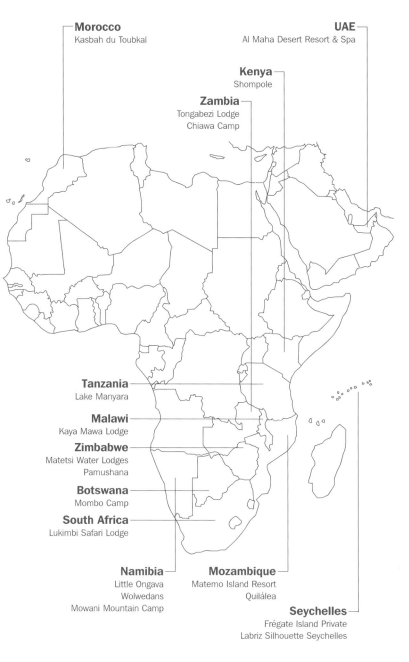

Morocco
Kasbah du Toubkal

UAE
Al Maha Desert Resort & Spa

Kenya
Shompole

Zambia
Tongabezi Lodge
Chiawa Camp

Tanzania
Lake Manyara

Malawi
Kaya Mawa Lodge

Zimbabwe
Matetsi Water Lodges
Pamushana

Botswana
Mombo Camp

South Africa
Lukimbi Safari Lodge

Namibia
Little Ongava
Wolwedans
Mowani Mountain Camp

Mozambique
Matemo Island Resort
Quilálea

Seychelles
Frégate Island Private
Labriz Silhouette Seychelles

Kasbah du Toubkal

Address:	Kasbah du Toubkal, BP 31, Imlil, Asni, Marrakech, Morocco
Phone:	+33 466 458 395
Fax:	+33 466 458 473
Website:	www.kasbahdutoubkal.com
e-mail:	kasbah@discover.ltd.uk
Located:	at the foot of Jbel Toubkal (4,165 m) 1,800 m above sea level, 60 km from Marrakech
Style:	Morrocan Kasbah style
Special features:	hammam, conference & event facilities for up to 100 people, trekking, ski mountaineering
Rooms:	11 rooms, 3 Berber salons
Opening date:	ruin rebuilt in the 1990s
Architecture / Design:	John Bothamley

Al Maha Desert Resort & Spa

Address:	Al Maha Head Office, 3rd Floor, Emirates Holidays Building, Sheikh Zayed Road, P.O. Box 7631, Dubai, United Arab Emirates
Phone:	+971 4343 9595
Fax:	+971 4343 9696
Website:	www.al-maha.com
e-mail:	almaha@emirates.com
Located:	in desert landscape, 45-minute drive from Dubai
Style:	traditional Bedouin encampment
Special features:	dining room, lounge, bar, library, swimming pool, executive boardroom for 20 people
Rooms:	43 suites
Opening date:	1999
Architecture / Design:	Rashid Taqui Schuster Pechthold + Partners Wrenn Associates

Frégate Island Private

Address: Frégate Island Private, Seychelles, Indian Ocean
Phone: +49 610 250 1321
Fax: +49 610 250 1322

Website: www.fregate.com
e-mail: sales@fregate.com

Located: 20-minute flight from Mahé
Style: classic tropical design
Special features: 2 restaurants, 2 bars, 7 beaches, 2 swimming pools, The Rock Spa, library
Rooms: 16 villas for a maximum of 40 guests

Opening date: 1998

Architecture / Design: Wilson & Associates

Labriz Silhouette Seychelles

Address:	Labriz Silhouette Seychelles, P.O. Box 69, Mahé, Seychelles
Phone:	+248 225 005, reservations +960 333 22 70
Fax:	+248 321 221
Website:	www.labriz-seychelles.com
e-mail:	reservations@labriz-seychelles.com
Located:	45-minute boat or 15-minute helicopter transfer from Seychelles Intl. Airport in the capital Mahé
Style:	modern, celebrates the environment, embodies the spirit of Seychelles
Special features:	restaurants, spa, fitness center, tennis court, water sports, café, library, museum, art gallery, boutique, Silhouette Giant Tortoise Sanctuary
Rooms:	17 pavilions, 63 beach villas, 30 garden villas
Opening date:	2006
Architecture / Design:	Harry Tirant, Tirant Associates Seychelles Bent Severin & Associates Pte Ltd Singapore

Shompole

Address:	Ngong View End, Off Ngong Road, Karen, Nairob Kenya
Phone:	+254 2088 3331
Fax:	+254 208 883 332
Website:	www.shompole.com
e-mail:	reservations@theartofventures.com
Located:	on the edge of the Nguruman Excarpment in a privat conservancy 120 km south of Nairobi
Style:	contemporary natural style with touch of African bush
Special features:	water flowing into private pools, no air-conditioning, restaurant, massages, biking, hiking
Rooms:	6 tented rooms, 2 suites
Opening date:	2001
Architecture / Design:	Anthony Russell Neil Rocher Elizabeth Warner

Lake Manyara

Address: Private Bag X 27, Benmore, 2010 Johannesburg, South Africa
Phone: +27 11 809 4300
Fax: +27 11 809 4400

Website: www.ccafrica.com
e-mail: information@ccafrica.com

Located: in the heart of a mahogany forest, in Lake Manyara National Park in northern Tanzania
Style: African style, crafted from timber and palm fronds
Special features: privacy of the location ensures near exclusivity of game-drives in the southern section of Lake Manyara National Park, open 4x4 safari vehicles great diversity of habitats, lakeshore picnics
Rooms: 10 stilted tree house suites

Opening date: 2002

Architecture / Design: Nicky Plewman
Chris Browne

Mombo Camp

Address:	Wilderness Safaris, P.O. Box 5219, Rivonia, 212 South Africa
Phone:	+27 11 807 1800
Fax:	+27 11 807 2110
Website:	www.wilderness-safaris.com
e-mail:	enquiry@wilderness.co.za
Located:	on Mombo Island in Okavango Delta in northern Botswana
Style:	camp architecture in African style
Special features:	tents and walkways raised off the ground, dining room, pub, swimming pool, game drives
Rooms:	9 rooms
Opening date:	1998
Architecture / Design:	Will Sutton and Andrew Came, with participation from the local community

Kaya Mawa Lodge

Address: Wilderness Safaris, P.O. Box 5219, Rivonia, 212
South Africa
Phone: +27 11 807 1800
Fax: +27 11 807 2110

Website: www.wilderness-safaris.com
e-mail: enquiry@wilderness.co.za

Located: in the south-west of Likoma Island, in the north
of Lake Malawi, close to Mazambique coast,
access by air or boat
Style: African style, built entirely by hand, consisting o
stone and teak-framed thatched cottages
Special features: dining room, bar, rock pool, water sports, visits
to the local villages, trips to Mozambique
Rooms: 8 rooms

Opening date: 1998

Architecture / Design: Will Sutton and Andrew Came,
with participation from the local community

Matemo Island Resort

Address: Matemo Island, Qurimbas Archipelago, Cabo Delgado Province, Mozambique
Phone: +27-11-467 1277
Fax: +27-11-465 8764

Website: www.matemoresort.com
e-mail: reservations@raniresorts.com

Located: in the Quirimbas Archipelago off the coast of northern Mozambique
Style: traditional African style with Arabian features
Special features: water sports, whale and dolphin watching, village tours
Rooms: 24 thatched chalets

Opening date: 2004

Architecture / Design: Architect – RSL
Interior Design – Nikki McCarthy Interiors

Quilálea

Address:	Quilalea Island, Quirimbas, Cabo Delgado Province, Mozambique
Phone:	+258 2722 1808
Fax:	+258 2722 1808
Website:	www.quilalea.com
e-mail:	info@quilalea.com
Located:	island in the Quirimbas Archipelago off northern Mozambique
Style:	traditional African style with handcrafted timber and rock walls, furniture in creole Muani style
Special features:	restaurant, lounge, water sports, bird watching
Rooms:	9 villas
Opening date:	2002
Architecture / Design:	Marjolaine Hewlett

Little Ongava

Address: Wilderness Safaris, P.O. Box 5219, Rivonia, 2128
South Africa
Phone: +27 11 807 1800
Fax: +27 11 807 2110

Website: www.wilderness-safaris.com
e-mail: enquiry@wilderness.co.za

Located: along the southern boundary of the Etosha
National Park in northern Namibia
Style: natural African style with camp and colonial
features
Special features: private camp, suites with swimming pool, view
over waterhole, near to main lodge
Rooms: 3 rooms

Opening date: 2003

Architecture / Design: Neil Hays
Ann Christopher

Wolwedans

Address: P.O. Box 5048, Windhoek, Namibia
Phone: +264 6123 0616
Fax: +264 6122 0102

Website: www.wolwedans.com
e-mail: info@wolwedans.com.na

Located: in the heart of Namib Rand Nature Reserve, 70 km south of Sossusvlei, nestled in red dune
Style: lodge in camp style architecture and a camp with dome-shaped tents on wooden platforms
Special features: 2 dining rooms, 2 lounges, wine cellar, swimmin pool, fireplace, library
Rooms: Dune Lodge with 9 chalets and 1 suite, private Camp with 2 bedrooms and Dune Camp with 6 tents on wooden platforms

Opening date: Dune Camp 1994, Dunes Lodge 1999 (reopene 2003 after fire), Private Camp 2001

Architecture / Design: Stephan Brückner

Mowani Mountain Camp

Address: Twyfelfontein, Namibia
Phone: +264 61 232 009
Fax: +264 61 222 574

Website: www.mowani.com
e-mail: mowani@visionsofafrica.com.na

Located: between the Ugab and Huab rivers, in Twyfelfontein Conservancy amongst huge boulders
Style: East-African
Special features: Restaurant, lounge, bar, pool
Rooms: 12 tents on wooden platforms with veranda, all with en suite facilities, 1 luxury room, 1 suite

Opening date: 2000

Architecture / Design: André Louw

Tongabezi Lodge

Address: Private Bag 31, Livingstone, Zambia
Phone: +260 332 4450
Fax: +260 332 4468

Website: www.tongabezi.com
e-mail: reservations@tongabezi.com

Located: on the banks of the Zambezi River just upstream
of the Victoria Falls
Style: natural, open African cottage style
Special features: boating, fishing, hiking, game drives, village
tours, health & beauty treatments
Rooms: 6 cottages, 1 honeymoon house, 1 bird house,
1 dog house, 1 tree house

Opening date: 1990

Architecture / Design: Will Ruck-Keene
Ben Parker

Chiawa Camp

Address: P.O. Box 30972, Lusaka, Zambia
Phone: +260 126 1588
Fax: +260 126 2683

Website: www.chiawa.com
e-mail: info@chiawa.com

Located: on the banks of the Zambezi River, in the heart
of Zambia's Lower Zambezi National Park
Style: open African style safari tents
Special features: lounge with upstairs deck, viewing point up in
a Mahogany tree, swimming pool, bush walks,
game drives, river safaris
Rooms: 9 tents

Opening date: 1989

Architecture / Design: Artillery Architecture & Interior Design of Londo
with Judi Helmholz and Grant & Lynsey Cuming
of Zambia

Matetsi Water Lodge

Address: CC Africa, Private Bag X27, Benmore 2010, South Africa
Phone: +27 11 809 4300
Fax: +27 11 809 4400

Website: www.ccafrica.com
e-mail: reservations@ccafrica.com

Located: along 15 km Matetsi's private Zambezi River frontage, 40 km upstream from Victoria Falls, in northwestern Zimbabwe
Style: elegant African safari style with colonial features
Special features: private plunge pools, gift shop, water activities, game viewing, birdwatching, adventures at nearby Victoria Falls
Rooms: 18 suites in 3 separate water camps

Opening date: 1996

Architecture / Design: Chris Browne

Pamushana

Address:	Shop 37, Arundel Shopping Center, Quorn Avenue, Harare, Zimbabwe
Phone:	+263 436 9136
Fax:	+263 436 9523
Website:	www.pamushana.com
e-mail:	mctsales@africaonline.co.zw
Located:	in Malilangwe Private Wildlife Reserve, 45-minute drive from Chiredzi in the south east of Zimbabwe
Style:	lodges in eco-style architecture built with intricate hand-hewn stone work, exotic works of art and richly textured materials from all over Africa
Special features:	dining room, swimming pool, gym, sauna, game drives, canoeing, hiking, fishing
Rooms:	6 villas
Opening date:	1998
Architecture / Design:	Bruce Stafford Cecile & Boyd

Lukimbi Safari Lodge

Address:	P.O. Box 2617, Northcliff, 2115, South Africa
Phone:	+27 118 883 713
Fax:	+27 118 882 181
Website:	www.lukimbi.com
e-mail:	res@lukimbi.com
Located:	in the southern part of the Kruger National Park
Style:	modern African decor, lodges connected with raised walkways
Special features:	dining room, bar, wine cellar, library, swimming pool, lounge, gym, business facilities, game drives
Rooms:	14 suites
Opening date:	2002
Architecture / Design:	Gareth Herbert of J-D Maresch Architects

Asia & Pacific

Maldives
India
China
Thailand
Australia
New Zealand
Fiji Island

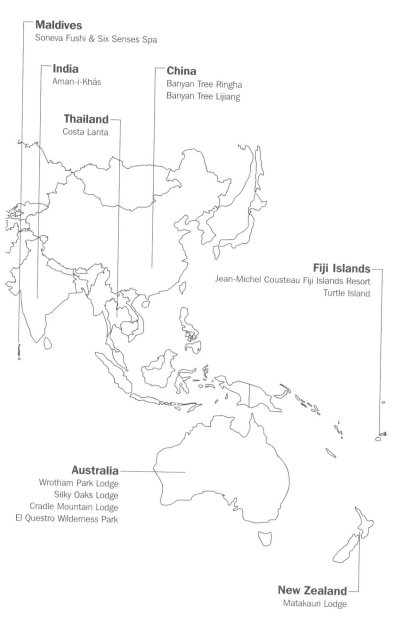

Maldives
Soneva Fushi & Six Senses Spa

India
Aman-i-Khás

China
Banyan Tree Ringha
Banyan Tree Lijiang

Thailand
Costa Lanta

Fiji Islands
Jean-Michel Cousteau Fiji Islands Resort
Turtle Island

Australia
Wrotham Park Lodge
Silky Oaks Lodge
Cradle Mountain Lodge
El Questro Wilderness Park

New Zealand
Matakauri Lodge

Soneva Fushi & Six Senses Spa

Address: Kunfunadhoo Island, Baa Atoll,
Republic of Maldives
Phone: +960 660 0304
Fax: +960 660 0374

Website: www.sixsenses.com
e-mail: reservations-fushi@sonevaresorts.com

Located: Soneva Fushi, in the North Baa Atoll region of
the Maldives
Style: "Robinson Crusoe" style combining natural,
stylish and traditional features
Special features: 2 restaurants, 2 bars, wine cellar, library, shops,
spa treatments, fitness center, tennis court,
biking, water sports
Rooms: 65 villas and suites

Opening date: 1995

Architecture / Design: based on a concept by Sonu & Eva
Shivdasani (owners)

Aman-i-Khás

Address:	Ranthambhore, Rajasthan, India
Phone:	+91 746 225 2052
Fax:	+91 746 225 2178
Website:	www.amanresorts.com
e-mail:	aman-i-khas@amanresorts.com
Located:	on the fringe of Ranthambhore National Park, in Rajasthan, India
Style:	tent camp in Mughal style, structure of steel frames, separations by fine cotton canvas, set up for 7 months of the year
Special features:	1 dining tent, 1 lounge tent, 1 spa tent, fireplace, game drives and walks, camel safaris
Rooms:	10 tents
Opening date:	2003
Architecture / Design:	Jean Michel Gathy

Banyan Tree Ringha

Address:	Hong Po Village, Jian Tang Town 674400, Diqing Tibetan Autonomous Prefecture, Yunnan Province, People's Republic of China
Phone:	+86 887 828 8822
Fax:	+86 887 828 8911
Website:	www.banyantree.com/ringha
e-mail:	ringha@banyantree.com
Located:	in China's Yunnan province, 50-minute flight to Shangri-La Airport from Kunming Intl. Airport
Style:	original, rustic Tibetan farmhouses and a lodge at 3.200 m above see level in shangri-la county
Special features:	3 restaurants, Banyan Tree Spa, treks and 4-wheel drive tours
Rooms:	32 lodges and suites
Opening date:	2005
Architecture / Design:	Architrave Design and Planning

Banyan Tree Lijiang

Address:	P.O. Box 55, Lijiang 674100, Yunnan Province, People's Republic of China
Phone:	+86 888 533 1111
Fax:	+86 888 533 2222
Website:	www.banyantree.com/lijiang
e-mail:	lijiang@banyantree.com
Located:	northwest of Yunnan Province, 2,400 meters above sea level, 40 minutes from Lijiang Airport
Style:	traditional Naxi architecture
Special features:	Bai Yun Chinese Restaurant, bar, tea lounge, Banyan Tree Spa
Rooms:	55 villas
Opening date:	2006
Architecture / Design:	Architrave Design and Planning

Costa Lanta

Address: 212 Moo 1 Saladan, Amphur Koh Lanta Krabi, Thailand
Phone: +66 2662 3550
Fax: +66 2260 9067

Website: www.costalanta.com
e-mail: info@costalanta.com

Located: in the south of Thailand, 80 km from Krabi airport, 80 km from Trang
Style: natural and minimalistic architecture, open and stylish concrete cubes
Special features: restaurant, bar, swimming pool
Rooms: 22 bungalows

Opening date: 2002

Architecture / Design: Duangrit Bunnag Architect Ltd. (DBALP)

Voyages Wrotham Park Lodge

Address:	Via Chillagoe, Queensland, Australia
Phone:	+61 282 968 010
Fax:	+61 292 992 103
Website:	www.wrothampark.com.au
e-mail:	travel@voyages.com.au
Located:	in Far North Queensland, 300 km west of Cairns
Style:	timber slab houses in Queensland's outback architecture
Special features:	restaurant, bar, lounge, swimming pool, horseback riding, station runs 35,000 cattle, seasonal cattle mustering
Rooms:	10 guest quarters
Opening date:	2004
Architecture / Design:	Pike Withers

Voyages Silky Oaks Lodge

Address:	3 Finlayvale Road, Mossman, Queensland, Australia
Phone:	+61 282 968 010
Fax:	+61 2 92 992 103
Website:	www.silkyoakslodge.com.au
e-mail:	travel@voyages.com.au
Located:	in the Daintree rainforest in tropical North Queensland, 20 minutes from Port Douglas
Style:	tropical eco-style architecture with natural tones and timbers
Special features:	restaurant, lounge, spa, gym, hiking, biking, tennis, golf, snorkeling, canoeing, horseback riding, conference facilities
Rooms:	50 rooms
Opening date:	1985
Architecture / Design:	Collin Talent and Gary Hunt Moss and Theresa Hunt

Voyages Cradle Mountain Lodge

Address:	Cradle Mountain Road, Cradle Mountain, Tasmania, Australia
Phone:	+61 282 968 010
Fax:	+61 292 992 103
Website:	www.cradlemountainlodge.com.au
e-mail:	travel@voyages.com.au
Located:	in the Tasmanian wilderness in Cradle Mountain/Lake St. Clair National Park, 80 km from Devonport
Style:	natural eco-style design, Tasmanian contemporary wood furnishing
Special features:	restaurant, lounge, bar, wine cellar, spa, hiking, biking, fishing, canoeing
Rooms:	86 cabins
Opening date:	1971
Architecture / Design:	Pike Withers

El Questro Wilderness Park

Address: Gibb River Road, The Kimberly, Western Australia
Phone: +61 282 968 010
Fax: +61 292 992 103

Website: www.elquestro.com.au
e-mail: sales@elquestro.com.au

Located: in the Kimberley region in north western Australia
Style: natural eco-style design with rustic turnishing, timber and stone bungalows
Special features: working cattle station with 5,000 cattles, restaurant, bar, swimming hole, hiking, boating, tours, also camping site
Rooms: 16 bungalows

Opening date: 1991

Architecture / Design: Geoffery Pie
Celia Burrell

Matakauri Lodge

Address:	Glenorchy Road, P.O. Box 888, Queenstown 9197, New Zealand
Phone:	+64 3441 1008
Fax:	+64 3441 2180
Website:	www.matakauri.co.nz
e-mail:	relax@matakauri.co.nz
Located:	among bush on the edge of Lake Wakatipu, 10-minute drive from Queenstown
Style:	contemporary timber houses
Special features:	dining room, wine cellar, library, spa, gym, winter sports
Rooms:	4 villas, 2 suites
Opening date:	1999
Architecture / Design:	Marc Scaife Sue and Graeme Shaw

Jean-Michel Cousteau
Fiji Islands Resort

Address: Savusavu, Fiji Islands
Phone: +1 415 7885794
Fax: +1 415 7880150

Website: www.fijiresort.com
e-mail: info@fijiresort.com

Located: on Fiji's 2nd largest Island Vanua Levu, overlooking Savusavu Bay, 7 km from Savusavu town
Style: Fijian bures/bungalows built of local timbers, thatch & bamboo reeds
Special features: dining room, bar, spa, massages, swimming pool, tennis, situated on a coconut plantation
Rooms: 25 bures

Opening date: 1985

Architecture / Design: Karen Taylor

Turtle Island

Address: Placencia Peninsula, Placencia Village, Stann Creek District, Belize

Phone: 360 256 4347 Local

Fax: 360-253-3934

Website: www.turtlefiji.com

Located: private island located on the famous Blue Lagoon

Style: traditional, thatched cottages in Fijian bure style

Special features: restaurant, wines, massage, horseback riding, hiking, water sports

Rooms: 14 bures

Opening date: reopened 2000

Architecture / Design: Richard Evanson

Photo Credits

Dana Allen, Little Ongava (278–283); **Andreas Burz**, Wolwedans (284–291), Mowani Mountain Camp (Cover, 292–297); **Bob Gevenski**, Hix Island House, A Vieques Hotel (79–83); **Gavin Jackson**, Pousada Picinguaba (140–147), Post Ranch Inn (20–25); **Lisa Linder**, Villa Fontelunga (174–179); **Martin Nicholas Kunz**, Hotelito Desconocido (106–113), Al Maha Desert Resort & Spa (229–235), Frégate Island Private (236–241), Anse Chastanet Resort (84–85, 87–91); **Chris McClennan**, Jean-Michel Cousteau Fiji Islands Resort (389, 391); **Doc Ross**, Matakauri Lodge (382–387); **Barbara Rowell**, Jean-Michel Cousteau Fiji Islands Resort (392); **Ric Wallis**, Jean-Michel Cousteau Fiji Islands Resort (388); **James Walshe**, Jean-Michel Cousteau Fiji Islands Resort (390); **Guy Wenborne**, Explora en Atacama (152–159)

Courtesy: Al Maha (228); Aman Resorts (332–339); Anse Chastanet (86); Banyan Tree Hotels & Resorts (340–351); Ca's Xorc (198–203); CC Africa (254–257, 312–315); Chiawa Camp (306–311); Costa Lanta (352–357); Don Enrique Lodge (136–139); Dräger (190–197); El Capitan Canyon (26–31); Francis Ford Coppola's Blancaneaux Resorts (122–129); Hix Island House (78); Hotel Punta Islita (130–135); Inkaterra (148–151); Island Outpost (56–71); Kasbah du Toubkal (224–227); Lake Placid Lodge (32–37); Lone Star (46–49); Lukimbi Safari Lodge (320–325); Montpelier Plantation Inn (72–77); Naturhotel Waldklause (168–173); Necker Island (50–55); Pamushana (316–319); Plan resorts SA (92–97); Post Ranch Inn (24); Quilálea (274–277); Rani Resorts (268–273); Shompole (248–253); Silhouette (242–247); Six Senses (328–331); Son Bernadinet (204–213); Son Gener (214–221); Starwood Hotels & Resorts (100–105); The Point (38–45); Tongabezi Lodge (298–305); Turtle Inn (114–121); Turtle Island (394–397); Vigilius Mountain Resort (180–189); Voyages (3; 358–381); Wilderness Safaris (258–261, 262–267); Yunak Evleri (162–167)

Other Designpocket titles by teNeues:

African Interior Design 3-8238-4563-2
Airline Design 3-8327-9055-1
Asian Interior Design 3-8238-4527-6
Bathroom Design 3-8238-4523-3
Beach Hotels 3-8238-4566-7
Berlin Apartments 3-8238-5596-4
Boat Design 3-8327-9054-3
Café & Restaurant Design 3-8327-9017-9
Car Design 3-8238-4561-6
Cool Hotels Second Edition 3-8327-9105-1
Cool Hotels Africa/Middle East 3-8327-9051-9
Cool Hotels America 3-8238-4565-9
Cool Hotels Asia/Pacific 3-8238-4581-0
Cool Hotels Cool Prices 3-8327-9134-5
Cool Hotels Europe 3-8238-4582-9
Cool Hotels Romantic Hideaways 3-8327-9136-1
Cosmopolitan Hotels 3-8238-4546-2
Country Hotels 3-8238-5574-3
Food Design 3-8327-9053-5
Furniture Design 3-8238-5575-1
Garden Design 3-8238-4524-1
Italian Interior Design 3-8238-5495-X
Kitchen Design 3-8238-4522-5
London Apartments 3-8238-5558-1
Los Angeles Houses 3-8238-5594-8
Miami Houses 3-8238-4545-4
New Scandinavian Design 3-8327-9052-7
Pool Design 3-8238-4531-4
Product Design 3-8238-5597-2
Rome Houses 3-8238-4564-0
San Francisco Houses 3-8238-4526-8
Shop Design 3-8327-9104-3
Ski Hotels 3-8238-4543-8
Spa & Wellness Hotels 3-8238-5595-6
Sport Design 3-8238-4562-4
Staircase Design 3-8238-5572-7
Sydney Houses 3-8238-4525-X
Tropical Houses 3-8238-4544-6
Wine & Design 3-8327-9137-X

Each volume:

12.5 x 18.5 cm, 5 x 7 in.
400 pages
c. 400 color illustrations